All Things Oreo

Delicious Recipes Featuring Your Favorite Cookie!

BY: Allie Allen

Copyright 2019 Allie Allen

Copyright Notes

This book is written as an informational tool. While the author has taken every precaution to ensure the accuracy of the information provided therein, the reader is warned that they assume all risk when following the content. The author will not be held responsible for any damages that may occur as a result of the readers' actions.

The author does not give permission to reproduce this book in any form, including but not limited to: print, social media posts, electronic copies or photocopies, unless permission is expressly given in writing.

Table of Contents

Introduction 6

1. Oreo Cake with Oreo Cream Frosting 8

2. Oreo Milkshake 12

3. Oreo Brownies 14

4. Oreo Mousse 17

5. Oreo Truffles 20

6. Oreo Ice cream 22

7. Oreo Pancakes 24

8. Oreo Sugar Cookies 27

9. Oreo Meringues 30

10. Oreo Popsicles 32

11. Oreo Cheesecake 34

12. Oreo Fudge 37

13. Oreo Krispies 39

14. White Chocolate Oreo Popcorn 41

15. Oreo Butter 43

16. Oreo Cupcakes 45

17. Oreo Crepes 49

18. Oreo Hot Chocolate 52

19. Oreo Waffles 54

20. Oreo Brownie Trifle 56

21. Oreo Muffins 60

22. Oreo Bark 63

23. Oreo Blondies 65

24. Oreo Lava Cakes 68

25. Oreo Cheesecake Cookies 71

26. Oreo Snack Mix 74

27. Oreo Caramel-Dipped Apples 76

28. Oreo Clusters 79

29. Oreo Bread Pudding 81

30. Oreo Granola 83

Conclusion 85

About the Author 86

Author's Afterthoughts 88

Introduction

Looking for ways to use up all those Oreos you stocked up on? Look no further than this ultimate Oreo recipe book! You'll find a variety of Oreo-filled recipes that are super easy to make and super delicious. Each recipe comes with a simple list of ingredients, easy-to-follow directions and the amount of time needed. The recipes can be easily doubled, tripled or even halved (but who would want to do that?).

By the end of this book, you will learn 30 different ways to use up Oreos, ranging from classic recipes like Oreo cupcake and milkshake to new favorites like Oreo bread pudding and Oreo butter. So gather up your Oreos and let's get started!

1. Oreo Cake with Oreo Cream Frosting

Moist, creamy and crunchy, this cake is chockful of Oreo goodness and is topped with an insanely delicious Oreo cream frosting.

Makes: 4-6 servings

Prep: 20 mins

Cook: 25 mins

Ingredients:

For the cake:

- 1 1/3 cups white sugar
- 1/3 cup vegetable oil
- 2 large eggs
- 2 tsp. vanilla extract
- 1/3 cup sour cream
- 1 2/3 cups all-purpose flour
- 1/2 + 1/8 tsp. salt
- 2/3 cup + 3 tbsp. milk
- 1 1/3 cup Oreos, crushed

For the frosting:

- 1 ½ cups heavy cream
- 3 tbsp. icing sugar
- ¾ tsp. vanilla extract
- 10 Oreo cookies, crushed, plus extra for topping

Directions:

For the cake:

Preheat the oven to 350°F. Line and grease 2 8-inch baking pans and set aside.

Using a hand mixer, beat together the sugar, oil, eggs and vanilla extract in a large bowl on medium-high speed for about 3 minutes or until pale. Add in the sour cream and beat until well combined.

Next, lower the speed and add in half of the flour followed by the baking powder and salt. Add in half of the milk and mix until just combined. Add in the remaining flour and then milk and beat until well combined. Lastly, fold in the crushed Oreos.

Decide batter evenly between the 2 cake pans and bake for about 25 minutes or until a toothpick inserted into the center of the cake comes out clean.

Place cakes on a cooling rack and let them cool completely.

For the frosting:

Using a hand mixer or stand mixer fitted with the whip attachment, beat together the heavy cream, icing sugar and vanilla extract in a large bowl until stiff peaks form. Fold in the crushed Oreo cookies.

Frost the cooled cakes and garnish with additional crushed Oreos.

Serve and enjoy!

2. Oreo Milkshake

A thick, cold and creamy Oreo milkshake recipe that is perfect for the summer months!

Makes: 6 servings

Prep: 5-10 mins

Cook: -

Ingredients:

- 4 1/2 cups vanilla ice cream
- 3 cups whole milk
- 24 Oreo cookies
- 4 tbsp. dark chocolate chips
- Whipped Cream, to serve
- Mini Oreos, to serve

Directions:

Place vanilla ice cream, whole milk, Oreo cookies and chocolate chips in a blender and blend until smooth.

Divide between glasses and serve topped with whipped cream and mini Oreos.

Enjoy!

3. Oreo Brownies

Thick, fudgy and stuffed with Oreos, these brownies are decadent and only require a few ingredients.

Makes: 32 brownies

Prep: 20 mins

Cook: 35 mins

Ingredients:

- 2 ½ sticks unsalted butter
- 3 cups white sugar
- 1 ½ cups cocoa powder
- ½ tsp. salt
- 4 large eggs, cold
- 4 tsp. vanilla extract
- 1 cup all-purpose flour
- 1 cup semi-sweet or dark chocolate chips
- 32 Oreo cookies
- 10 Oreo cookies, chopped

Directions:

Preheat your oven to 350°F. Line a 16x16 inch baking pan with baking paper.

In a microwave-safe bowl, heat the butter, cocoa powder, sugar and salt for 1 minute. Stir and heat again for another minute.

Whisking constantly, add the eggs and vanilla extract next and mix until combined. Then, gently add in the flour followed by the chocolate chips and mix until just combined.

Pour half the batter into the prepared pan and top with the 32 Oreo cookies. Pour the remaining batter onto the cookies and top with chopped Oreos.

Bake for 35 minutes. Let the brownies cool completely on a cooling rack before slicing and serving.

Enjoy!

4. Oreo Mousse

Soft, velvety and rich, this Oreo mousse is simple to make and decadent enough to be served at any party.

Makes: 8 servings

Prep: 20 mins plus chilling time

Cook: -

Ingredients:

- 16 Oreo cookies, crushed
- 16 Oreo cookies, whole
- 2 tbsp. milk
- 2 tbsp. unsalted butter, melted
- ½ cup heavy cream
- 2 cups semi-sweet or dark chocolate chips
- 2 cups whipped cream

Directions:

Lightly grease the bottom of an 8x8 inch baking pan. Spread the crushed Oreos evenly onto the pan.

In a small bowl, combine the melted butter and milk and drizzle it over the crushed Oreos.

In a microwave-safe bowl, combine the chocolate chips and heavy cream and heat in 20 second intervals until all the chocolate has melted. Set aside to cool.

Once cooled, transfer mixture to a large bowl. Gently fold in the whipped cream until well combined.

Pour in half of the mousse mixture onto the pan and top with 8 whole Oreos. Pour the remaining half on top, cover and refrigerate for at least 3 hours.

Serve with remaining Oreos and enjoy!

5. Oreo Truffles

Delicious chocolate balls made with crushed Oreos and cream cheese and dipped in chocolate. These make the perfect edible gift!

Makes: 2 dozen truffles

Prep: 30 mins plus chilling time

Cook: -

Ingredients:

- 4 oz. cream cheese, softened
- 18 finely Oreos, crushed, divided
- 6 oz. dark chocolate chips

Directions:

In a medium-sized bowl, combine 1 ½ cups of crushed Oreo with the cream cheese. Scoop mixture into 1-inch balls and place on a baking sheet lined with wax paper. Place in the freezer for 10 minutes.

In the meantime, melt the chocolate chips in the microwave in 20 second intervals. After the 10 minutes are up, dip each ball into the melted chocolate and place back on the baking sheet. Refrigerate for an hour or until firm.

Serve and enjoy!

6. Oreo Ice cream

Only 5 ingredients are needed for this delicious Oreo-filled vanilla ice cream.

Makes: 12 servings

Prep: 15 mins plus freezing time

Cook: -

Ingredients:

- 1 cup whole milk, cold
- 2/3 cup white sugar
- 2 cups heavy cream, cold
- 2 tsp. vanilla extract
- 1 cup Oreos, crushed

Directions:

In a large bowl, mix together the cold milk and sugar for 1 minute. Add in the heavy cream and vanilla extract and mix again until well combined.

Transfer mixture into ice cream maker and freeze according to instructions provided by manufacturer.

Add in the crushed Oreos and stir until combined. Transfer to a loaf pan and freeze for about 2 hours.

Serve and enjoy!

7. Oreo Pancakes

An indulgent and easy breakfast (or dessert) recipe that comes with a creamy whipped Oreo cream.

Makes: 15 pancakes

Prep: 30 mins

Cook: 45 mins

Ingredients:

For the pancakes:

- 1 ½ cups all-purpose flour
- 1 tsp. baking soda
- ½ cup unsweetened cocoa powder
- 2 tsp. baking powder
- ½ tsp. salt
- ¾ cup white sugar
- 2 cups buttermilk
- 2 eggs
- 6 tbsp. unsalted butter, melted
- 12 Oreos, crushed

For the Oreo cream:

- 3 cups heavy cream, cold
- ½ cup white sugar
- 4 Oreos, crushed

Directions:

In a large bowl, combine the flour, cocoa, baking powder, salt, baking soda and sugar using a whisk. Next, add in the eggs, buttermilk and melted butter and whisk again until just combined. Then, gently fold in the crushed Oreos. Let the mixture sit for a few minutes to thicken.

Lightly grease a skillet over medium heat. Pour ¼ cup of batter onto the skillet or griddle and cook for a minute or until bubbles start to form on the surface. Flip and cook the other side until the pancake is cooked through. Then repeat with the remaining batter.

For the cream:

In a large bowl, using a hand whisk or a stand mixer, beat together the cream and sugar on high speed for 4 minutes or until stiff peaks form.

Pipe cream onto one of the pancakes, top with crushed Oreos and then place another pancake on top. Repeat until you have 3 stacks of 5 pancakes each.

Serve and enjoy!

8. Oreo Sugar Cookies

Soft, chewy and crackly sugar cookies stuffed with Oreo chunks. Say hello to your new favorite cookie!

Makes: 12 cookies

Prep: 15 mins

Cook: 15 mins

Ingredients:

- 1 cup all-purpose flour
- ¼ tsp. baking soda
- ¼ tsp. salt
- 5 Oreos, crushed into crumbs
- 1 stick unsalted butter, softened
- ½ cup brown sugar
- ¼ cup white sugar
- ½ tbsp. vanilla extract
- 1 egg
- 7 Oreos, roughly chopped

Directions:

In a medium-sized bowl, combine the flour, baking soda, salt and Oreo crumbs.

In a large bowl, using a hand mixer, beat the butter, white sugar and brown sugar for 2 minutes. Add in the eggs and vanilla extract and beat for another minute.

Next, add in the dry mixture and beat until just combined. Then, fold in the roughly chopped Oreos using a wooden spoon. Cover and refrigerate for an hour.

Preheat the oven to 350°F at least 10 minutes prior to taking the dough out of the fridge. Line a baking pan with baking paper.

Scoop out 1 tablespoon of cookie dough at a time and place on the baking sheet. Make sure the cookies are at least 3 inches apart. Bake for about 15 minutes or until the edges are slightly toasted.

Place on a cooling rack to cool completely.

Serve and enjoy!

9. Oreo Meringues

These delicious chewy meringue cookies require just 4 ingredients to put together!

Makes: 12

Prep: 10 mins

Cook: 45 mins

Ingredients:

- 4 large egg whites
- Pinch of salt
- ¾ cup white sugar
- 18 Oreos, crushed, plus additional for topping

Directions:

Preheat the oven to 275°F. Line a baking sheet with baking paper and set aside.

In a large bowl, using a hand mixer or stand mixer, whisk together the egg whites and salt until foamy. Add in the sugar, a tablespoon at a time, and whisk until firm and shiny peaks form. Gently fold in the crushed Oreos to create a swirl.

Pipe out or scoop 12 meringues onto the baking sheet and bake for about 50 minutes or until the meringues have dried out slightly.

Cool completely before serving.

Enjoy!

10. Oreo Popsicles

Creamy, cold and delicious Oreo popsicles that everyone will love!

Makes: 16 popsicles

Prep: 15 mins plus freezing time

Cook: 2 mins

Ingredients:

- 2 ½ cups heavy cream
- 1 ½ cups whole milk
- 1 cup white sugar
- 20 Oreos, divided

Directions:

In a large saucepan, combine together the cream and milk. Put the pan on the stove and heat on low. Add in the sugar and whisk for 1 minute or until all the sugar has dissolved. Remove from the heat set aside to cool slightly.

Crush 8 Oreos using a food processor and then add it to the cream mixture. Roughly break the remaining Oreos and again, add it to the cream mixture.

Pour the mixture into popsicle molds and place in the freezer to set for about 7 hours or overnight.

Enjoy!

11. Oreo Cheesecake

This light, creamy and easy cheesecake recipe comes with a delicious Oreo base and requires no baking whatsoever.

Makes: 10 servings

Prep: 5 hrs. 25 mins

Cook: -

Ingredients:

For the crust:

- 25 Oreos
- ¼ cup unsalted butter, melted

For the cheesecake:

- 16 oz. cream cheese, softened
- 1 cup icing sugar
- 1 tsp. vanilla extract
- 1 cup heavy whipping cream, cold
- 14 Oreos, chopped, plus extra for topping

Directions:

For the crust:

Place Oreos in a food processor and process to crumbs. Transfer to a bowl, add in the melted butter and mix until combined.

Scoop the mixture into a 9 inch springform pan and press until even. Place in the fridge to chill.

For the cheesecake:

In a large bowl, using a hand mixer or stand mixer, beat the cream cheese for 1 minute or until smooth. Add in the icing sugar and vanilla and beat until well combined.

In a medium-sized bowl, whip the heavy whipping cream for 3 minutes or until stiff peaks form. Gently fold it in to the cream cheese until just combined. Lastly, fold in the chopped Oreos.

Remove the pan from the fridge, pour in the cream cheese mixture and using a spatula, spread it around evenly. Sprinkle on additional chopped Oreos and press them slightly into the cheesecake.

Cover and refrigerate for 5 hours or overnight.

Enjoy!

12. Oreo Fudge

Sweet and toothsome white chocolate fudge with chunks of Oreo in every bite!

Makes: Approx. 3 dozen

Prep: 10 mins plus chilling time

Cook: 10 mins

Ingredients:

- 18 Oreos, roughly chopped, divided
- 1 14 oz. can sweetened condensed milk
- 2 tbsp. unsalted butter
- 2 2/3 cups white chocolate chips
- 1 tsp. vanilla extract

Directions:

Line an 8x8 inch baking pan with baking paper and spray with cooking spray. Place half of the crushed Oreos into the pan and set aside.

In a large saucepan, combine the condensed milk, butter and white chocolate chips over low heat. Stir and cook until all the chocolate chips have melted. Remove from heat and add in the vanilla extract.

Pour mixture over the Oreos in the pan and then sprinkle on the remaining Oreos on top. Cover and refrigerate for 2 hours.

Cut into squares and serve.

Enjoy!

13. Oreo Krispies

The classic Rice Krispie treat gets an Oreo twist thanks to this easy recipe. Thick, chewy and irresistible.

Makes: 6 servings

Prep: 10 mins plus chilling time

Cook: 5 mins

Ingredients:

- 2 ½ cups Krispies
- 8 Oreos, crushed
- 4 ½ cups mini marshmallows, divided
- 2 ½ tbsp. unsalted butter
- ¼ tsp. salt

Directions:

In a large bowl, combine the Krispies, crushed Oreos and ½ cup of mini marshmallows.

In a large saucepan, melt the butter over medium heat. Add in the remaining mini marshmallows and salt and cook until all the marshmallows have melted. Then, pour the mixture into the Oreo mixture and gently fold with a spatula until evenly combined.

Spread the mixture into a 6x6 inch pan and press gently with the spatula.

Let the mixture cool for at least half an hour before slicing.

Enjoy!

14. White Chocolate Oreo Popcorn

Skip the regular buttered popcorn and try this delicious white chocolate and Oreo popcorn instead. Sweet and crunchy, this is the ultimate snack recipe!

Makes: 12 servings

Prep: 10 mins

Cook: -

Ingredients:

- 10 cups popped popcorn
- 24 Oreos, crushed
- 18 oz. white chocolate chips

Directions:

Place popped popcorn and crushed Oreos in a large bowl and set aside.

Melt the white chocolate chips in the microwave in 20 second intervals. Pour over the popcorn and Oreos and mix together until evenly coated.

Allow the popcorn to cool and then serve.

Enjoy!

15. Oreo Butter

Spread this luscious butter on your morning toast for an indulgent and delicious breakfast treat.

Makes: 1 jar of Oreo butter

Prep: 15 mins

Cook: -

Ingredients:

- 36 Oreos
- 3 tbsp. coconut oil

Directions:

Place Oreos and coconut oil in a food processor and process for 5 minutes. Scrape down the sides and process again for 5 more minutes.

Transfer butter into a jar and let it cool to room temperature.

Enjoy!

16. Oreo Cupcakes

Delicious and moist Oreo cupcakes with a whipped cream Oreo frosting and a whole Oreo at the bottom.

Makes: 8 cupcakes

Prep: 15 mins

Cook: 18 mins

Ingredients:

For the cupcakes:

- ¾ cup all-purpose flour
- 1/8 tsp. salt
- ¾ tsp. baking powder
- ¼ tsp. baking soda
- ¼ cup brown sugar
- ¼ cup + 2 tbsp. white sugar
- ½ tsp. vanilla extract
- 6 tbsp. vegetable oil
- ½ cup buttermilk
- ½ cup + 2 tbsp. Oreos, chopped
- 8 Oreos, whole
- 1 egg

For the frosting:

- 1 ½ cups heavy cream
- 3 tbsp. icing sugar
- ¾ tsp. vanilla extract
- 10 crushed Oreo cookies, plus extra for garnish

Directions:

Preheat oven to 350°F. Line a cupcake pan with cupcake liners and set aside.

In a medium-sized bowl, combine together the flour, salt, baking powder and baking soda.

In a large bowl, using a hand whisk or a stand mixer, beat together the egg and sugars for 3 minutes or until pale. Add in the oil and vanilla and beat until combined. Next, add in 1/3rd of the flour mixture followed by ½ of the buttermilk and beat again until combined. Repeat with remaining flour mixture and buttermilk. Lastly, fold in the chopped Oreos.

Place an Oreo on the bottom of each cupcake liner. Divide the batter evenly between the cupcakes and bake for 18 minutes or until a toothpick inserted into the center comes out clean.

Place cupcakes on a cooling rack to cool completely.

For the frosting:

Using a hand mixer or stand mixer fitted with the whip attachment, beat together the heavy cream, icing sugar and vanilla extract in a large bowl until stiff peaks form. Fold in the crushed Oreo cookies.

Frost the cooled cupcakes and garnish with additional crushed Oreos.

Serve and enjoy!

17. Oreo Crepes

Indulge in these cream-filled Oreo crepes for breakfast or dessert.

Makes: 6 servings

Prep: 5 mins

Cook: 10 mins

Ingredients:

- 2 cups milk
- 3 eggs
- 1 cup all-purpose flour
- 3 Oreos, crushed
- 1 cup heavy cream
- 1 ½ tbsp. icing sugar
- 20 Oreos, chopped

Directions:

In a large bowl, whisk together the eggs and milk. Add in the flour and crushed Oreos and whisk until well combined.

Spray a medium-sized non-stick pan with cooking spray and heat over medium heat. Pour about 2 ½ tbsp. of batter into the pan and swirl to cover the base. Cook for 2 minutes or until slightly golden. Flip crepe and cook for a minute more. Transfer to a plate and repeat with remaining batter.

In a medium-sized bowl, combine the heavy cream, sugar and Oreos.

Spread about 1/3 cup of cream mixture onto each crepe, fold in half and then serve.

Enjoy!

18. Oreo Hot Chocolate

Beat the winter blues with a cup of this rich, thick and creamy Oreo hot chocolate.

Makes: 4 servings

Prep: 5 mins

Cook: 5 mins

Ingredients:

- 10 Oreos, crushed into fine crumbs, plus additional for topping
- 2 cups milk, divided
- 1 cup heavy cream
- 1 ½ tsp. cornstarch
- 6 oz. dark chocolate chips

Directions:

In a large saucepan, combine 1 ½ cups milk and cream. In a small bowl, whisk together remaining milk and cornstarch until well combined. Add it to the pan and whisk again.

Cook on medium low for about 4 minutes or until bubbles start to appear around the edge. Remove from heat, add in the chocolate chips and crushed Oreos and whisk until well combined. Pass through a strainer if desired to get a smoother texture.

Divide between mugs and enjoy!

19. Oreo Waffles

Crispy on the outside and soft on the inside, these scrumptious Oreo waffles will quickly become your favorite breakfast recipe.

Makes: 12 servings

Prep: 10 mins

Cook: 20 mins

Ingredients:

- 3 cups all-purpose flour
- ¼ cup unsweetened cocoa powder
- ¼ cup white sugar
- 2 tsp. baking powder
- ¾ cup milk
- 4 eggs
- 4 tbsp. unsalted butter, melted
- 20 Oreos, crushed, plus additional for topping
- Whipped cream, for topping

Directions:

In a large bowl, whisk together all the ingredients except Oreos until smooth. Then, fold in the crushed Oreos.

Spray your waffle maker with a cooking spray and cook waffles according waffle maker instructions.

Serve with whipped cream and additional crushed Oreos.

Enjoy!

20. Oreo Brownie Trifle

With layers of brownie, whipped cream, chocolate pudding and Oreo crumbs, this recipe is a guaranteed crowd pleaser!

Makes: 12 servings

Prep: 10 mins

Cook: 40 mins

Ingredients:

For the brownies:

- 1 20oz. box dark chocolate brownie mix
- 2 eggs
- 1 tbsp. milk
- ½ cup vegetable oil

For the pudding:

- 1 3.5 oz. box instant chocolate or Oreo pudding mix
- ½ cup water
- 1 tsp. vanilla extract
- 1 14 oz. can sweeten condensed milk
- For the trifle:
- 3 cups heavy whipping cream, divided
- 14 Oreos, crumbled

Directions:

For the brownies:

Preheat oven to 325°F. Grease a 9x9 inch baking pan and set aside.

In a large bowl, whisk together the brownie mix, oil, eggs and milk. Pour into the prepared pan and bake for about 35-40 minutes or until a toothpick inserted comes out clean. Set aside to cool.

For the pudding:

In a large bowl, whip the heavy whipping cream for 3 minutes or until soft peaks form.

In another large bowl, combine together the pudding mix, vanilla extract, water and condensed milk. Then, fold in half of the whipped cream.

To assemble the trifle:

Once the brownies have cooled, cut them into 1 inch squares.

In a large glass serving dish or bowl, place half of the brownies, half of the pudding, half of the remaining whipped cream and half of the crumbled Oreos. Repeat and then cover and refrigerate for 3 hours.

Serve and enjoy!

21. Oreo Muffins

Moist, fluffy and delicious, these Oreo muffins are a perfect breakfast, snack or dessert option.

Makes: 6 servings

Prep: 15 mins

Cook: 15 mins

Ingredients:

- ¾ cup + 2 tbsp. all-purpose flour
- 1 cup white sugar
- ½ tbsp. baking powder
- ¼ tsp. salt
- 2 tbsp. unsalted butter, cut into small cubes
- 1 small egg or ½ a large egg
- ½ cup milk
- 8 Oreos, chopped

Directions:

Preheat the oven to 400°F. Line a muffin pan with 6 muffin liners.

In a large bowl, combine together the sugar, baking powder, flour and salt. Add in the butter with your hands or a pastry blender and mix until mixture resembles crumbs.

In a small bowl, beat together the egg and milk until well combined. Add it to the flour mixture and mix until the crumbs are just moistened. Gently fold in the Oreos.

Spoon mixture evenly into the muffin liners and bake for 15 minutes or until a toothpick inserted comes out clean.

Place on a cooling rack to cool slightly.

Serve and enjoy!

22. Oreo Bark

A simple 2-ingredient dessert recipe that is perfect for the holidays. Give as a gift or eat it all yourself!

Makes: 16 servings

Prep: 10 mins plus chilling time

Cook: 3 mins

Ingredients:

- 20 oz. good-quality white chocolate chips
- 30 Oreos, chopped, plus extra for topping

Directions:

Line a 16x16 inch baking pan with wax paper and leave a 1 inch overhang on both sides.

Place chocolate chips in a microwave-safe bowl and melt in 20 second intervals. Alternately, chocolate chips can be melted in a double boiler. Cool for 5 minutes, then add in the chopped Oreos and stir until combined.

Pour mixture into the baking pan and smooth out the top. Add additional chopped Oreos on top. Refrigerate for 30 minutes or until the chocolate has set. Lift the bark out of the pan and break in pieces.

Enjoy!

23. Oreo Blondies

These chewy, Oreo-stuffed blondies taste even better the next day with your morning cup of coffee.

Makes: 16 servings

Prep: 10 mins

Cook: 25 mins

Ingredients:

- 2 cups + 2 tbsp. all-purpose flour
- ¾ tsp. salt
- ½ tsp. baking soda
- 1 cup white sugar
- ½ cup brown sugar
- 2 eggs
- 1 tsp. of vanilla extract
- ¾ cup unsalted butter, melted
- 1 cup Hershey's cookies and cream chocolate, chopped
- 1 cup Oreos, chopped
- Ice cream, to serve

Directions:

Preheat the oven to 325°F. Lightly grease a 9x13 inch baking pan set aside.

In a medium-sized bowl, combine together the flour, salt and baking powder.

In a large bowl, whisk the butter, white sugar and brown sugar until well combined. Add in the eggs, one at a time, followed by the vanilla extract and whisk until well combined. Then, add in the flour mixture and whisk until just combined. Lastly, fold in the chopped chocolate and Oreos.

Pour mixture into the prepared pan and bake for 25 minutes or until the edges are golden-brown. Cool blondies in the pan for 15 minutes and then transfer to a cooling rack to cool completely.

Serve with ice cream and enjoy!

24. Oreo Lava Cakes

Warm and moist dark chocolate cakes with an Oreo pudding lava center. Delicious!

Makes: 8 servings

Prep: 30 mins

Cook: 18 mins

Ingredients:

- ½ cup instant Oreo pudding mix
- 1 cup milk, cold
- 2 cups dark chocolate, chopped
- 1 ½ cups milk
- 1 cup all-purpose flour
- 2 tsp. baking powder
- ¼ cup vegetable oil
- Vanilla ice cream, to serve

Directions:

In a small bowl, whisk together the Oreo pudding mix and cold milk until well combined and smooth. Set aside for 10 minutes to thicken.

Preheat the oven to 350°F. Grease eight 4oz. ramekins and dust generously with flour. Tap ramekins to remove excess flour.

In a large microwave-safe bowl, combine the chocolate chips and milk. Melt chocolate in 20 second intervals until smooth. Add in the remaining ingredients and whisk until well combined.

Pour mixture into the ramekins until they are half full. Then, scoop 2 tbsp. of pudding into the center of each ramekin. Top evenly with remaining batter.

Place ramekins onto a baking pan or sheet and bake for 18 minutes or until the surfaces of the lava cakes are just set. Remove and run a knife around the sides of each of the cakes. Place a plate on top of a ramekin and using a kitchen mitt, invert quickly to release the cake from the ramekin. Repeat with remaining cakes.

Serve with ice cream and enjoy!

25. Oreo Cheesecake Cookies

Why choose between cheesecake and cookies when you can have both? This recipe gives you a delicious hybrid of two of the most amazing desserts ever.

Makes: 12 cookies

Prep: 15 mins

Cook: 20 mins

Ingredients:

- 1 stick unsalted butter, softened
- 3 oz. cream cheese, softened
- 1 tsp. vanilla extract
- 1 cup white sugar
- 1 cup all-purpose flour
- ½ cup mini dark chocolate chips
- 1 cup Oreos, crumbled

Directions:

Preheat the oven to 375°F. Line a large baking pan with baking paper.

In a large bowl, using a hand mixer or stand mixer, beat the softened cream cheese and butter for 1 minute until creamy. Add in the vanilla and sugar and beat until well combined. Gently fold in the flour and chocolate chips.

Scoop out the dough and roll into a ball. Roll the dough in the crushed Oreo crumbs and coat well. Place on baking sheet and repeat with remaining dough.

Bake for 12 minutes. Cool for 5 minutes in the pan before transferring onto a rack to cool completely.

Enjoy!

26. Oreo Snack Mix

This Oreo fruit-and-nut mix is the perfect snack to nibble on when boredom strikes. It's also super versatile!

Makes: 4 cups

Prep: 5 mins

Cook: -

Ingredients:

- 16 Oreos, chopped
- 1 bag potato chips
- 1 cup mixed nuts
- 1 cup dried cranberries

Directions:

Combine all the ingredients in a large bowl.

Store in an airtight box or serve.

Enjoy!

27. Oreo Caramel-Dipped Apples

Caramel-dipped apples become gourmet delights when covered in a crunchy Oreo coating, then drizzled with white chocolate.

Makes: 6 servings

Prep: 20 mins plus standing time

Cook: 10 mins

Ingredients:

- 6 wooden pop sticks
- 6 large apples
- 20 oz. caramels
- 3 tbsp. water
- 24 Oreos, chopped
- 6 oz. white chocolate
- 2 tsp. vegetable oil

Directions:

Skewer the stem end of each apple and insert the wooden sticks in. Set aside.

Heat caramels and water in a large saucepan over medium-low heat, stirring until mixture is smooth.

Dip apples into melted caramel and spoon to coat. Roll in chopped Oreos and press gently to coat. Place on baking sheet and let stand for 25 minutes or until caramel sets.

Heat chocolate and oil in a medium-sized saucepan over low heat, stirring until melted and smooth. Cool for 15 minutes. Drizzle over apples and let stand until firm.

Enjoy!

28. Oreo Clusters

This delicious and fun recipe uses mini Oreos, marshmallows and nuts to give you the ultimate Oreo snack.

Makes: 2 ½ dozen

Prep: 20 mins

Cook: -

Ingredients:

- 1 8oz. package Mini Oreos
- 1 cup mini marshmallows
- ¾ cup almonds
- 8 oz. semi-sweet chocolate, melted

Directions:

Line a baking pan with wax paper. Set aside.

Combine cookies, marshmallows and almonds in a large bowl.

Drizzle melted chocolate over cookie mixture and stir until well coated.

Drop rounded tablespoonfuls of cookie mixture onto the baking pan. Refrigerate for 10 minutes or until hardened. Remove from waxed paper and serve.

Enjoy!

29. Oreo Bread Pudding

Transform your old bread into a warm, chocolatey Oreo pudding.

Makes: 12 servings

Prep: 15 mins

Cook: 50 mins

Ingredients:

- 8 cups day-old bread cubes
- 32 Oreos, chopped
- 4 cups milk
- 1 cup sugar
- ½ cup unsalted butter, melted
- 2 tsp. vanilla extract
- 4 eggs

Directions:

Preheat the oven to 350°F.

In a large bowl, mix bread cubes and chopped Oreos and set aside.

In a medium-sized bowl, combine milk, sugar, butter, eggs and vanilla. Add it to the bread mixture and stir until evenly coated. Pour mixture into a 3-quart round casserole.

Bake for 45 minutes or until set. Serve.

Enjoy!

30. Oreo Granola

Keep plenty of this crispy granola on hand to top ice cream or oatmeal, or to simply munch on as a satisfying snack.

Makes: 5 cups

Prep: 10 mins

Cook: 25 mins

Ingredients:

- 2 cups rolled oats
- ½ cup flaked coconut
- ½ cup pecans, chopped
- 3 tbsp. honey
- 4 tsp. orange juice
- 16 Oreos, chopped

Directions:

Preheat the oven to 300°F.

Combine together the oats, coconut, pecan, honey and orange juice in a large baking pan.

Bake or 15 minutes. Remove and stir and then bake for 10 minutes more. Cool.

Add in the chopped Oreos and mix until well combined.

Enjoy!

Conclusion

There you have it! 30 different and delicious ways to use Oreos! Make sure to try all of them and share with your friends and family!

About the Author

Allie Allen developed her passion for the culinary arts at the tender age of five when she would help her mother cook for their large family of 8. Even back then, her family knew this would be more than a hobby for the young Allie and when she graduated from high school, she applied to cooking school in London. It had always been a dream of the young chef to study with some of Europe's best and she made it happen by attending the Chef Academy of London.

After graduation, Allie decided to bring her skills back to North America and open up her own restaurant. After 10 successful years as head chef and owner, she decided to sell her business and pursue other career avenues. This monumental decision led Allie to her true calling, teaching. She also started to write e-books for her students to study at home for practice. She is now the proud author of several e-books and gives private and semi-private cooking lessons to a range of students at all levels of experience.

Stay tuned for more from this dynamic chef and teacher when she releases more informative e-books on cooking and baking in the near future. Her work is infused with stores and anecdotes you will love!

Author's Afterthoughts

I can't tell you how grateful I am that you decided to read my book. My most heartfelt thanks that you took time out of your life to choose my work and I hope you find benefit within these pages.

There are so many books available today that offer similar content so that makes it even more humbling that you decided to buying mine.

Tell me what you thought! I am eager to hear your opinion and ideas on what you read as are others who are looking for a good book to buy. Leave a review on Amazon.com so others can benefit from your wisdom!

With much thanks,

Allie Allen

Made in the USA
Columbia, SC
14 May 2023